Growing Through

AF624498

Brianna Brookes

BookLeaf Publishing

Presentation by *BookLeaf Publishing*

Web: www.bookleafpub.com

E-mail: info@bookleafpub.com

ISBN: 9789357211208

First edition 2022

DEDICATION

For my husband-

Who's support and patience is endless. I love you always. Apples and orchards.

For my son-

All the words in all the languages are not enough to describe my love for you. You can't read yet, but when you can I suggest reading something else.

For my Grandma -

All those trips to the bookstore, prompts and talks as a teen didn't leave me. I hope I make you proud.

PREFACE

This collection of poetry isn't for the faint of heart. It's for those who understand how complex love, life and trauma can be.
It's most definitely not for those who know me.

If I could

If I could I'd hold you.
If wrap the cuts on your wrist
get on my knees and pray beside you.
I'd acknowledge the words you never spoke
and feel the ones you were brave enough to
shout

No one will ever save you
but I'd walk those stones with you.
If you knew then where it would lead
I'm not sure it would actually change anything
but I can guarantee
It would feel less lonely
If I could
I'd tell you we end up okay.
I would

State of Mind

Damaged is as damaged does
That's why I like a damaged fuck
I told my therapist I was damaged
She asked, "Why"
I said, "I'm broken inside."

Never had a friend that was stable
Every one had a "broken glass" label.
When you seek out bad it makes you worse.

Damaged demons coming knocking
the clock won't stop fucking tocking
There's a Devil in my ear
Beckoning "Come here."
I live in the threshold.

Faded

They faded, the cuts on my wrist
so has the memory of people I've kissed
You pushed me to lick
paper
run lines
get fucked out my mind
Maybe that's why
I live off lies
Can't value devotion
Haunted by the notion
that I can never be
Happy.

Day Like Before

There was nothing unusual about that night,
I came from work and didn’t want to fight.
But there was a strange man in the living room
and you had a short fuse.
You raised your hand and I just ran.
Ran to sanctuary next door
so that night wasn’t like the ones before
something inside me broke.
I refused to be hit anymore.

Afraid

It's no surprise how scared I am
You can only be cornered so many times,
exploited and oppressed
hear the yelling,
glass shattering,
sheetrock cracking
take the choking,
punching,
pushing
before fear is ingrained
of everyone and everything
because people are all the same.
I hope my son never knows how aggressive the world can be
because nightmares of my own life still plague me.

I'm Sorry

It keeps me up at night.
The times I've failed
The times I've bailed
I promise I did my best
Even at my own expense

Even when I wanted to die
When I was out of mind terrified
I could never leave you
You kept me alive

I have my scars
you have yours
I just wanted you to know
I did everything I could

How

How fast does your high horse run?
How high is the pedestal you live on?
If God held a black light to your hands how dirty would they be?
How much weed have you smoked, how many pills have you popped, how many bottles have you emptied?
Don't worry you don't have to answer
I already know
I'm waiting for the day your world goes up in smoke.

Karma

You should be scared of me
I learned from you
All the things a person should never do
Do you know what it’s like to be you
Or not really, since you’re split in two?
I feel like I’m on fragile ground.
It's breaking under you now.
Come down from there, time to bow.

Pretend

If we play pretend
we can act like you were everything I needed
life was good and I was happy
I was safe and wanted
I'll finally be loved

Nice to meet you

Say hello, shake my hand, tell me how pretty I
am.
You'll regret your existence shortly after
I can make you feel like the dirt under my feet if
you do the same
I love the pain
but only if you do too

Average

Tell me you love me
Pull me close to your skin
Tell me how your fighting your demons
and need me to win
Tell me I'm a goddess
That's you being modest
Tell me how I'm your everything
and you'll do anything
Tell me how you fucked up
Guess what
You're not to blame
All you fuckers are the same.

Join the Club

There's honey in your smile
Lead weights in your hands
Privilege in your hair
Porcelain in your ego
Ramen in your pants
Kindergarteners in your lies
No antidote to your words
Technicolor smile that'll dazzle the girls
They'll get sucked in just like me
I'll be on the ground
licking my wounds at your feet.

Confetti

It’s heaven when you whisper hellish things
Make wet spots and bite back screams
Goosebumps on my skin
Make it happen again
I want the marks permanent
the position intimate
confetti imminent

Puff Puff Past

You taste like citrus and my lips
Honey laced kiss
Imprint of your fingerprints
Start a fire
Love a liar
Pass the blunt
Do what you want
Tainted by you
Obsessed with you
Undressed by you
If only you
could feel what I do.

Dumpster Diver

There's times when I can still smell your
cologne
It'll take me back to how your arms felt
how your fingers would fit with mine.
All of our moments pass
but never let go.
You never leave me completely.
I know why you're stuck in my head
but it's hard to imagine why you can't let go
either.
If I treated you like you did me
I wouldn't be worth a memory
So why do you keep coming back
If only to discard me so quickly again?
But I discarded you too
So who's to say we're both not trash
that just keeps ending up in the same dumpster.

Liable for Life

I always know how to hurt myself
Ruin a good time
Make a bad choice worse
Liable to destroy my own life
I can’t trust myself to do what I need.
If it’s up to me
I’ll demolish everything.

Dust for Ground

This time feels different
You won’t meet my eyes
I really fucked up this time.
Every time before I've reeled you back
I don’t know if this time it’ll happen like that.
I always thought I didn’t deserve you
but the way you’re avoiding my eyes now
makes me think you finally know it too.
I wanna reach out, say something, touch
but the eggshells under my feet are turning to
dust.

Cuddle Companion

I can’t sleep.
Fear chokes me
too many regrets,
a masochistic game.
Which tragedy will kill me tonight?
What nightmare memory will lay beside me,
curl up next to me,
whisper sadistic nothings in my ear
until it consumes me,
leaving me discarded, bruised
drowning in its weight.

Domesticated

I’m fickle and flighty
Easily swayed
Easily stolen away
I promise I’ve changed
I’m no longer that way
I’m not a flight risk
I’m cuffed at the wrist
I’ve settled down
Look around
It's domesticated life now

Bugabaloo

I wish I could go back to those feedings around
the clock
just humming to you while we rock
then you run to me and I want to stay here
forever
every day your getting better

I remember when your hair was fine
now its curlier than mine
Every second you're smarter and bigger
Every growth spurt coming quicker

You hazel eyes are a perfect mix of daddy’s and
mine
your smile makes my world shine

Every day

Every night since you were born I've rocked you to sleep.
I sing or read poetry.
mostly I just look at you.
Look at your precious face
Try to commit it to memory.
Tomorrow you'll be another day older, you'll have grown a bit more.
You'll face will never look the same as the day before
You'll say a new word, walk faster, reach higher.
Every day you change but every night I rock you to sleep and it feels every bit the same as that very first day.

www.ingramcontent.com/pod-product-compliance
Lightning Source LLC
Chambersburg PA
CBHW051720130826
49812CB00034B/1266
* 9 7 8 9 3 5 7 2 1 1 2 0 8 *